D0333182

CHANGING
GEOGRAPHY

SERIES EDITOR: **JOHN BALE**

Disability, space and society
ROB KITCHIN

Geographical
Association

ACKNOWLEDGEMENTS

I would like to thank John Bale, Phil Hubbard, Steve Royle, Shelagh Waddington and two anonymous reviewers for useful and constructive comments on an earlier draft of this book. I would also like to thank members of the Disability and Geography International Network for providing a constructive environment in which to discuss the issues the text addresses.

The Geographical Association would like to thank the following individuals and organisations for offering advice and supplying some of the images used in this book:

- Peter Wright at Birmingham City Council's Department of Planning and Architecture

- The Leonard Cheshire Foundation

- The Royal National Institute for the Blind and the JMU Access Partnership for supplying and permission to reproduce the images on page 22. The JMU Access Partnership is a pan disability Access Consultancy jointly supported by the Royal National Institute for the Blind and the Guide Dogs for the Blind Association.

AUTHOR: Dr Rob Kitchin is a lecturer in the Department of Geography, National University of Ireland, Maynooth, County Kildare, Ireland.

ISBN 1 899085 87 4
First published 2000
Impression number 10 9 8 7 6 5 4 3 2 1
Year 2003 2002 2001

Published by the Geographical Association, 160 Solly Street, Sheffield S1 4BF. The Geographical Association is a registered charity: no 313129.

The Publications Officer of the GA would be happy to hear from other potential authors who have ideas for geography books. You may contact the Officer via the GA at the address above.

Edited by Rose Pipes
Designed by ATG Design, Catalyst Creative Imaging, Leeds
Printed and bound in Hong Kong by Colorcraft Ltd.

CONTENTS

EDITOR'S PREFACE

The books in the *Changing Geography* series seek to alert students in schools and colleges to current developments in university geography. It also aims to close the gap between school and university geography. This is not a knee-jerk response – that school and college geography should be necessarily a watered-down version of higher education approaches – but as a deeper recognition that students in post-16 education should be exposed the ideas currently being taught and researched in universities. Many such ideas are of interest to young people and relevant to their lives (and school examinations).

The series introduces post-16 students to concepts and ideas that tend to be excluded from conventional school texts. Written in language which is readily accessible, illustrated with contemporary case studies, including numerous suggestions for discussion, projects and fieldwork, and lavishly illustrated, the books in this series push post-16 geography into the realm of modern geographical thinking.

This book focuses on an area that has attracted a good degree of geographical interest in recent years: the links between geography and disability. Traditionally, geography explored the world through 'ableist' perspectives. Yet, as Rob Kitchin demonstrates, geography is central to the lives of disabled people and geographical principles can be applied to issues surrounding disability. *Disability, space and society* tackles issues of discrimination and human welfare and shows how geography itself can 'disable' people through the configurations of urban areas. This is a stimulating book that will alert geography students both to the 'place' of disability and to a wide range of learning activities that satisfy the requirements of post-16 examinations.

Disability, space and society will also be of use to students following courses in Sociology and Health and social care.

John Bale
August 2000

INTRODUCTION

Approximately one person in every six (15-18 per cent of the population) in Western societies is disabled[1]. You may be disabled yourself or you may have family members who are disabled. All of you will have seen disabled people (e.g. wheelchair users) at some point, either in real life or on the television, but have you ever seriously considered disability issues and the role of geography in disabled people's lives? Unless you are disabled, or help care for a disabled person, there may seem few reasons to contemplate disability issues in detail. However, there are a number of reasons why it is both an interesting and insightful exercise, in particular because of the relationship between geography and disability. Indeed, examining this relationship will:

- demonstrate why geography is an important element in understanding disability;
- reveal the types of practical problems disabled people face in their everyday lives and how we, as geographers, can offer potential solutions.
- help you understand society and your position within it;
- focus your thinking on a group to which many of you will one day belong, especially if you reach old age;
- highlight the ways in which some groups in society are disadvantaged and discriminated against.

This book is designed to help you think further about these and other disability issues and about the importance of geography in understanding, explaining and improving the lives of disabled people. To aid your learning, Information Boxes have been used to highlight specific issues in detail, and Activity Boxes offer practical activities designed to help your thinking on specific ideas.

1. Rates vary depending on how you measure disability and whether you include people aged over 65 and people who have chronic illness. It is generally agreed though that rates are somewhere between 10 and 18 per cent. The percentage of population also varies as a function of age. For example, about 5 per cent of children under the age of ten are disabled whereas 35 per cent of people over the age of 65 are disabled.

Photo: Leonard Cheshire.

CHAPTER 1

DEFINING DISABILITY

The category of people labelled by society as disabled is very diverse in nature. Rauscher and McClintock (1997, p. 199) identify the following disabilities as those which belong to the 'disabled' category:

- perceptual (such as visual and hearing impairments, learning disabilities);
- illness-related (such as multiple sclerosis, AIDS);
- physical (such as cerebral palsy);
- developmental (such as Down's Syndrome);
- psychiatric (such as chronic depression, manic-depressive syndrome);
- mobility (such as quadruplegia, paraplegia);
- environmental (such as asthma, sensitivities to allergens and chemicals in the environment).

The assumption on which the above list is based is that disability is a medical issue: thus the daily problems that disabled people face are understood and treated as being the direct result of their impairment (e.g. missing limb, no sight, differing mental ability). As such, the solution to the problems faced by disabled people is treatment and rehabilitation aimed at allowing them to overcome an impairment and to take part in 'normal' daily activities. This conception of disability forms the basis of the World Health Organisation's (WHO) definitions:

- to have an **impairment** is to be missing a body-part, or to have a defective body-part (manifested as, for example, paralysis, diabetes, mental retardation, nearsightedness)
- to have a **disability** is to experience difficulty in seeing, speaking, hearing, writing, walking, conceptualising or any other function within the range considered 'normal' for a human being
- a **handicap** is a disability which has interfered with the development of a person's capability to do what is normally expected at a certain age.

Here, there is a clear relationship between the concepts of impairment, disability and handicap. For example, if the impairment is nearsightedness, the disability is not being able to see distant objects clearly, and the handicap is a loss of orientation. If the impairment is skeletal, then the disability might be an inability to walk, therefore the handicap is a lack of mobility.

The WHO definition of disability, because it describes disability in relation to impairment, is said to represent a *medical model of disability*, and it is this model which determines how much of Western society views disability. It is used by government agencies to assess the needs and requirements of disabled people, and in surveys, such as the Census, to gauge the prevalence of people with disabilities and how impairments affect daily activities such as paid employment (e.g. through the calculation of how many disabled people work). However, the way that disability is defined and understood is changing and many people have rejected the medical model on the grounds that it does not fully take account of the experiences of disabled people or the role of society in disabling people with impairments. For example, Michael Oliver (1990) has argued that the medical model of disability is a theory of personal tragedy, where a disabled person is portrayed as an unfortunate individual; the victim of nature or fate. Together with other disabled writers Oliver has put forward a *social model of disability*, arguing that the vast majority of daily difficulties faced by disabled people are caused by society's failure to accept disabled people for who they are and provide adequate facilities for them. In other words, the problems faced by disabled people are not the result of their individual biology but the collective lack of acceptance and provision by society in general. Thus, in the social model the definitions of impairment and disability become as follows:

- to have an **impairment** is to be lacking part or all of a limb, or have a defective limb, organ or other body mechanism, or to have a less than fully developed mental ability
- to have a **disability** is to be disadvantaged or restricted in one's activities by a society which

takes insufficient account of people who have physical, sensory or mental impairments and thus to be excluded from mainstream social activities.

The difference between the medical and social model is illustrated by the questions in Information Box 1.The first question (MM) in each pair focuses on impairment and attributes the problem to the disabled person, while the second question (SM) focuses on society and its role in disabling a person with an impairment.

The social model is important because it forces us to reconsider the ways in which we think about and treat people. Once we start to deconstruct definitions

---

Information Box 1: Comparing the medical and social models of disability

To illustrate the differences between the medical and social model Michael Oliver (1990, pp. 8-9) compares questions asked by the Office of Population Censuses and Surveys in a survey designed to measure the extent of disability in the UK (medical model – MM) with an alternative set of questions designed by himself (social model – SM).

MM: Can you tell me what is wrong with you?
SM: Can you tell me what is wrong with society?

MM: What complaint causes you difficulty in holding, gripping or turning things?
SM: What defects in the design of everyday equipment like jars, bottles and tins causes you difficulty in holding, gripping and turning them?

MM: Are your difficulties in understanding people mainly due to a hearing problem?
SM: Are your difficulties in understanding people mainly due to their inability to communicate with you?

MM: Do you have a scar, blemish or deformity which limits your daily activities?
SM: Do other peoples' reactions to any scar, blemish or deformity you may have, limit your daily activities?

MM: Have you attended a special school because of a long-term health problem/disability?
SM: Have you attended a special school because of your education authority's policy of sending people with your health problem or disability to such places?

MM: Does your health problem/disability mean that you need to live with relatives or someone else who can help look after you?
SM: Are community services so poor that you need to rely on relatives or someone else to provide you with the right level of personal assistance?

MM: Did you move here because of a health problem/disability?
SM: What inadequacies in your housing caused you to move here?

MM: How difficult is it for you to get about your immediate neighbourhood on your own?
SM: What are the environmental constraints which make it difficult for you to get about in your immediate neighbourhood?

MM: Does your health problem/disability prevent you from going out as often or as far as you would like?
SM: Are there any transport or financial problems which prevent you from going out as often or as far as you would like?

MM: Does your health problem/disability make it difficult for you to travel by bus?
SM: Do poorly-designed buses make it difficult for someone with your health problem or disability to use them?

MM: Does your health problem/disability affect your work in any way at present?
SM: Do you have problems at work because of the physical environment or the attitudes of others?

Photo: Birmingham City Council, Department of Planning and Architecture.

conceptualisations of how society currently views and approaches disability in *practical* terms (see Table 1). The first two conceptualisations, medical and rehabilitation, draw from the medical model of disability and advocate *treatment*. The second two conceptualisations, independent living and interdependency, draw from the social model of disability and advocate *acceptance and independence*. Of course the reality is that some of the problems faced by disabled people are the result of their impairment and can be tackled by medical treatments and other strategies, and other issues are the result of how society is run and organised. The position taken in this book is that disability is a mix of both social and medical models, and the focus is on examining how the spatial organisation of society disables people; how geography is important in shaping disabled people's lives; and what geographers can do to help address specific problems.

of disability we discover that things are not as simple as they first seemed. People are not disabled or non-disabled, they belong somewhere on a continuum of abilities. Thus, for example, some people have better eyesight or hearing than others, some are good at sport and not at music, or vice versa. Our society, then, is very diverse in terms of abilities, experiences and attitudes and it is important to acknowledge this, as well as the fact that there are degrees of ability. How people with impairments are treated depends on the level and 'apparentness' of their impairment. Thus, a person with an eye impairment who needs to wear glasses is not treated the same way as someone who is totally blind (although both might receive differential treatment, such as name calling). In other words, how we define somebody has important implications for that person's experience of life.

Bob Bureau (Rausher and McClintock, 1997, p. 229) argues that the two models of disability, medical and social, have led to four different

Photo: Leonard Cheshire.

Activity Box 1: Thinking about disability

Revisit Table 1 and:

1. choose the approach which you think society should adopt in relation to disabled people;
2. write a short paragraph explaining why you think that this approach should be adopted.

Compile a tally of how many people in your class 'voted' for each approach.

Discuss as a whole class how people 'voted' and what the most popular choice might mean for disabled people.

Table 1: Conceptualising disability in practical terms

	Medical	Rehabilitation	Independent living	Interdependency
Definition of dilemma or problem	That a person has a physical, mental or emotional impairment.	Given their disability, the person lacks necessary job skills and needs rehabilitation.	Dependence on medical professionals, family, friends, and the community at large to get own needs met.	Historical distance from the heart of society. Viewed as broken, abnormal, and of no essential, genuine value.
Central issues of dilemma/ problem	The actual existence of the disability. That it must be eradicated if at all possible.	The person does not fit into society with their disability. They need to adjust/adapt to the situation.	The laws, values and attitudes of society are set up rigidly to enforce dependency and restrict freedom.	Dualistic society which acts to perpetuate categories of superior/inferior. The intentional oppression of disabled people.
Solution to dilemma/ problem	Research into curing the disability through surgery, drugs or invasive treatment.	Vocational rehabilitation, sheltered workshops, physical therapy, and adaptive technology.	Mutual support, self-help, removing all barriers. Cross-disability political action, and social change.	Shift control of available resources to people with disabilities. Empowerment and transformation.
Social role of person	Medical patient.	Rehabilitation patient.	Disabled person who consumes/uses services.	Respected and valued community member.
Expectations of person	Absolutely compliant with medical advice, submissive, never question authorities.	Grateful, eager to appear like everyone else, to be normal. Should complete treatment plan.	Assertive, retains sovereignty over own life, entitled to a full range of options/ choices.	Personal freedom, dignity in taking risks, learning, succeeding, creating, and even, at times, failing.
Group who control services	Traditional medical schools, licensed doctors who support drugs and surgery.	Funding sources, social service agencies, charities, foundations, and all levels of government.	Disabled people.	All disabled people, and their own genuine chosen community.
Goals and outcomes	To cure, to do everything possible to get rid of it, or at least to numb any existing pain.	Maximum adaptation to society, to be made as normal as possible, and to get a job.	Independent living in the community, on own terms.	Recognition that our world has tremendous social diversity, which must not be used to justify fearing or dehumanising anyone.

CHAPTER 2

GEOGRAPHY AND DISABILITY

Before the 1990s there were very few studies of the relationship between disability and geography, and only recently have geographers started to study this relationship systematically. As Information Box 2 illustrates, geography is implicated in the lives of disabled people in many different ways and many issues are in need of further investigation. Some of these issues relate to identifying and addressing how geography can disable people, and others relate to

providing practical solutions to particular problems (such as designing navigation aids for people with visual impairments). In the following chapters, both of these aspects are discussed in more depth, and case studies from the UK and Ireland are used to illustrate each topic.

Photos: Leonard Cheshire and Birmingham City Council, Department of Planning and Architecture.

Information Box 2: Disability issues examined by geographers

Planning and urban design issues
For example, examining (1) the ways in which the physical environment excludes disabled people by denying access to certain locations; (2) how to design environments that are accessible to disabled people (see Information Box 3, page 14 and Activity Boxes 2 and 3, pages 13 and 16, Case study 1, pages 17-20 and Information Box 8, page 40).

Mapping disability
For example, constructing maps of where people with different impairments are located and then seeing if there is any relationship with variables such as social conditions, pollution or type of environment (see Case study 1, pages 17-20).

Transport and mobility
For example, (1) examining how accessible transport is for disabled people; (2) measuring the spatial behaviour patterns of disabled people (how far disabled people travel, how frequently, by what means, etc.) (see Case study 2, pages 20-21).

Experiences of living within urban and rural environments
For example, asking disabled people about what it is like to live in a location and some of the issues that concern them (see Case study 3, pages 21-24).

Learning and communicating geographic information
For example, examining how people with visual impairments remember and learn spatial features such as street layout and the routes between locations either through direct experience or through secondary media such as tactile maps (see Case study 3: pages 21-24).

Access to labour markets and schooling
For example, examining, in terms of infrastructure and attitudes, the accessibility of labour markets and schooling to disabled people (see Case study 4, pages 24-26 and Case study 5, pages 26-28).

Moving people with developmental/psychiatric disabilities and mental illness out of institutions and into the community
For example, examining (1) community reactions to people who are released into the community from institutions such as asylums; (2) the spatial behaviour and spatial experiences of such people (see Case studies 5 and 6, pages 26-29).

Siting of mental health facilities, residents' reactions and the socio-economic effects
For example, examining the effects (social and economic) of siting mental health facilities in a particular location (see Case study 6, page 29 and Activity Box 14, page 38).

Historical geography of mental health facilities and conceptions of health and disability
For example, examining (1) how institutions and medical practice developed, and why they were located in certain places; (2) the ways in which our thinking about disability has changed over time and varies between cultures (see Case study 6, page 29).

Impact of health care reforms upon the availability and character of medical facilities
For example, examining (1) how changing government policy affects the locations of services; (2) facilities and the people who use them (longer/shorter journey times, etc.) (see Chapter 3, pages 13-31).

Cross-cultural comparisons
For example, examining the relationship between geography and disability in different places both in relation to legislation and actual provision (see pages 13-31).

HOW GEOGRAPHY DISABLES PEOPLE

'The human landscape can be read as a landscape of exclusion ... The simple questions we should be asking are: who are places for?, whom do they exclude?, and how are these prohibitions maintained in practice?' (Sibley, 1995, p. ix).

By taking the social model of disability and applying it to geographical concerns we can start to understand how the organisation of places disables people. For example, according to the medical model the inability of a wheelchair user to get into a building which has a stepped entrance is attributed to the fact that they cannot walk. However, according to the social model they cannot enter because of the use of steps. If a ramp is constructed the building becomes accessible to the wheelchair user. In other words, it is the steps that disable the wheelchair user, not the user's impairment.

There are many other ways in which geography disables people and makes it difficult for them to negotiate an environment. For example, it is common to find kerbs at crossings rather than dropped kerbs and tactile markings; cash machines that are too high for wheelchair users; and places linked by inaccessible public transport. Even where there is provision for disabled people it is often separate or different from non-disabled provision. For example, public toilets for disabled people are mostly separate from able-bodied toilets, and theatres and cinemas generally restrict wheelchair users to certain parts of the auditorium, usually towards the front or the sides. As such, the experiences of disabled and non-disabled people in trying to negotiate an environment are often very different, with the disabled person encountering many more problems of mobility (see Information Box 3 and Activity Box 2).

All of the problems detailed in Activity Box 2 can be tackled with relative ease. For example, steps can be complemented with a ramp, cash machines can be placed lower. What this reveals is that the built environment is rarely 'natural' but is the product of people's values and actions. Indeed the built

---

Activity Box 2: Thinking about access I

Take a walk around your local shopping centre and undertake an audit of:

- the proportion of disabled people to non-disabled people
- how people with physical and sensory impairments would get to the shopping centre
- how accessible the areas between the shops are for people with physical and sensory impairments
- how accessible, both from the street and once inside, the shops are to people with physical and sensory impairments
- how the shops provide for people with learning and developmental disabilities (e.g. visual signs, colour coding)
- how many specialised services are provided in the immediate area (e.g. shop mobility, accessible toilets)

If conducted as part of project work, photograph different environments and construct a poster depicting access in the shopping centre.

- What conclusions can you draw from your audit?

Tip: refer to Information Box 4 and Information Box 8 (page 40) which detail the sorts of things an access auditor would look for, and how they might undertake an audit.

Information Box 3: Types of inaccessible environment

Photos: Rob Kitchin and Newbridge Access Group.

environment does not just occur, it is carefully planned, so if we wanted to make accessible environments we could do so. The fact that many environments are not accessible for all is itself a statement on how we as a society view and value disabled people. To geographers such as Rob Imrie (1996), inaccessible environments suggest a form of 'design apartheid' whereby planners, architects and building control officers are guilty of constructing environments that 'lock' disabled people out. This occurs, he suggests, because planners and architects are mostly interested in how a building looks or how it will be used by the majority of users, and so fail to consider the needs of disabled people. The result is that environments and buildings are designed as if all people are the same (non-disabled). Imrie argues that those who build and shape the environments we live in need to re-think their designs in order to make society more inclusive.

Other geographers have considered the messages that inaccessible environments communicate to disabled people, arguing that what they convey to disabled people is that they are 'out of place' – they should not be there. As Napolitano writes:

'Good inclusive design will send positive messages to disabled people, messages which tell them: "you are important"; "we want you here"; and "welcome" … Often the way that disabled people are expected to get into a building is round the back, past the bins and through the kitchens, what does that message communicate? How will it make a disabled person feel?' (Napolitano, 1995, p. 33).

Here it is argued that the landscape is 'written' as a text, containing messages that we can read. We have all been taught how to create and read such messages, whether it is to be apprehensive when we walk down a dark alley or to be quiet in libraries. In other words, when we look at an environment we recognise whether we 'belong' there and can decide what is appropriate behaviour in that context. In the case of disability, geographers are interested in how landscapes reflect the values of the people who designed them and those of the people who live there. Geographers are also interested in how such designs and values affect disabled people – how disabled people feel when they are trying to negotiate inaccessible environments and how this affects their spatial behaviour (where they go). Such studies demonstrate that disabled people's spatial behaviour is not just affected by issues of accessibility but also by issues of acceptance, provision and attitudes. Understanding how geography disables people, then, is as much about understanding how the environment conveys messages of belonging and exclusion as it is about understanding the organisation and structure of places (see Activity Box 3).

How geography disables people is not just about badly planned environments or the messages they convey. Indeed, there are at least two other significant ways that geography is important in disabled people's lives, both of which relate to how society is organised and the provision of services.

First, it is recognised that how we operate as a society has spatial consequences. Thus, services such as social welfare provision have consequences in relation to people's daily travel patterns. Take the example of social care provision in the UK for people who need help with everyday activities such as dressing, washing and cleaning. Currently, this help is generally provided by the local authority or by relatives. Authority-provided care usually consists of 'helpers' coming several times a week to help with household chores such as cooking and cleaning. Usually visits are timetabled and set to a routine. As a consequence, spatial behaviour is restricted to modes of travel provided by the local authority (e.g. 'Dial-a-ride') and is limited both in time and distance. Trips outside the home usually have to be planned carefully in advance. Where a family member is the main carer, inadequate and infrequent support can place an intolerable burden upon the carer and severely restrict their spatial behaviour as well as that of the person they are caring for. In a study of the geography of caring within Glasgow, Christine Milligan (1997) has shown that carers are often tied to the site of caring, especially if they are the sole carer, with little time for a social life. Travel outside the home is usually restricted to places within walking distance of the site of care, or short car journeys to specific locations such as shops. In addition, provision of relief support by local authorities varies across districts because of priorities and patterns of spending. Geographical location, then, affects the level and extent of carer support (some people are literally the 'victims' of geography).

Second, society uses space in a very explicit way to create a particular geography – a geography of segregated and separate spaces. Such spaces include special schools, day-care units and sheltered workshops. Disabled people are encouraged or forced to live within these spaces to 'protect' the public from them, or vice versa. These spaces themselves convey messages and Rob Imrie (1996) suggests that they perpetuate discrimination against disabled people by labelling them as different, as needing specialised and

Activity Box 3: Thinking about access II

Below is an extract from Ben Elton's novel *Gridlock*. Read the extract and then answer the following questions:

1. How is the disabled person portrayed in the passage?
2. What sorts of access problems does Deborah encounter?
3. How does the text illustrate the ways in which geographic space is written?

Discuss your answers as a class.

Deborah [using a wheel chair because of a car accident] would come to realise that the only thing missing from doorways, steps, lifts, escalators, kerbs, etc., in London, were neat signs saying **ACHTUNG! No Disabled People Allowed** ... For Deborah, once a warm and vibrant human being, exuding personality and soul, had become a fire hazard. Fire hazard, and specifically a fire hazard. Not obstruction, embarrassment or damn nuisance, but fire hazard.

The reason Deborah was so specifically a fire hazard was that in those two little words, the abled-bodied community let itself off the hook. It would of course be churlish to deny someone access to a theatre or pub because their chair would be difficult to get up a flight of steps, or because they might occupy more space than walking customers and hence are less profitable. On the other hand, to deny someone access because they are a fire hazard – well, there is a sensible and public spirited action. There is a fast route to the moral high ground if ever there was one ...

Should Deborah, or anyone similarly afflicted be so selfish as to complain about their effective ostracism from social and cultural life, what would she be doing but wishing pain or death upon the abled-bodied community? And let us face it, it is not their fault that she is in a wheelchair.

'It's the possibility of a panic that worries us' people would patiently explain to Deborah. 'You have to ask yourself what your situation would be in the case of a rush or stampede.'

Very occasionally Deborah attempted to argue her corner, pointless though she knew it to be.

'Listen bud,' she had said, as politely as she could manage, to the slightly punky young man who was refusing to sell her a ticket to a play to be performed in an upstairs room of a pub ... 'It is Saturday afternoon OK? And I have just negotiated the entire length of Oxford Street. I dealt with it all; the tone deaf dickwit playing two of the three chords of "Blowin' in the wind", who kindly had his guitar case full of five pence bits spread across half the pavement ... I have got around ten broken paving stones that the council kindly put there to trip up blind people and snag wheelchairs. I have avoided the one-and-a-half million tourists standing in groups wondering how they just managed to pay five pounds for a can of coke.

I have circumnavigated the thousands of thugs from the city in pretend Armani suits who can't see you because they are so busy talking into their portable phones. So they bash you in the knees with their stupid brief-cases, with reinforced steel corners, that are absolutely essential to protect the bag of crisps and a copy of Penthouse, which is all they have inside the case.

I have detoured round the gangs of bored youths who hang around outside each and every one of the identical fast food outlets offering identical crap in a bag and Tennessee Fried Dog; the crocodile of French schoolgirls with their beautiful Benetton jumpers tied round their waists, just at a nice level to get caught in the face; the endless men who stop dead directly in front of me to turn round and look at the French schoolgirls' asses; the road works; the bollards; the steaming piles of plastic bin liners; the taxis taking a little known short cut along the pavement; the bloke who stands around with a sandwich-board saying eat less meat and protein; and the strange bearded tramp waving his arms around and screaming fuck off at everybody. All these things I have dealt with today, in a bloody wheelchair, bud. I think I could just about handle twenty-five assorted teachers and social workers making for the door in an upstairs pub!'

Source: Elton, 1992.

segregated facilities. This in turn suggests that because the disabled have their own geography we do not need to make *all* environments accessible for them. While many of these spaces provide valuable functions for disabled people, they could in fact be attached to similar facilities for non-disabled people. For example, many educationalists now argue that the provision of separate schools for disabled children has a number of negative effect: (such as children being ill-prepared for life beyond school), and offer only a narrow range of educational opportunities. It separates children from their peers both socially and geographically (schools are often outside of the local community), reinforces attitudes that disabled people are different, and ties up resources that need to be spread between children

who have a range of abilities. In short, the system is one of 'them and us', failing to recognise the broad spectrum of educational abilities. Attaching the special school to a mainstream school, and letting disabled and non-disabled children share the same environments (e.g. the playground), if not the classroom, provides an opportunity for all children to mix and to learn about one another (see pages 26-28). In other words, inclusion would highlight similarities and promote understanding and interaction. This approach is adopted in some countries, for example, in Spain and Italy there are no special schools.

In summary, it is clear that geography greatly influences disabled people's lives. This is illustrated in greater detail by the case studies that follow.

Case study 1: Access to the built environment

A number of geographers have examined issues of access to the built environment. For example, Peter Vujakovic and Hugh Matthews (1994) examined the wheelchair accessibility of Coventry. They used a partnership approach to achieve their aims, pairing wheelchair users (consultants) with geographers (mappers). Initially, both the wheelchair users and the geographers drew sketch maps of routes between locations in Coventry city centre (Figure 1). These maps were then compared and contrasted. It

immediately became clear that wheelchair users had to use less direct and longer pathways to reach the same destinations as non-wheelchair users. By comparing maps, areas of inaccessibility could be identified. Using the findings, both groups collaborated to produce an accessibility map of Coventry accompanied by a mobility index. The final map revealed how disabled people are disabled through urban planning and design (Figure 2). A similar exercise was recently completed in relation to

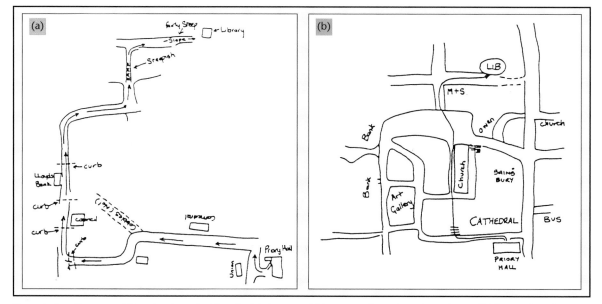

Figure 1: Cognitive maps of Coventry, drawn by (a) a wheelchair user, and (b) a geography undergraduate. Source: Vujakovic and Matthews, 1994.

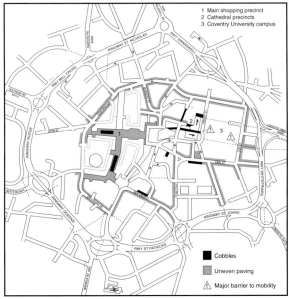

Figure 2: An extract from the collaboratively-produced access map of Coventry. Source: Vujakovic and Matthews, 1994.

Newbridge, Ireland, and the results of the survey were plotted on a 1:1250 scale map using the symbols displayed in Information Box 4 (Figure 3 shows an extract from the final map). The photographs in Information Box 3 on page 14 show the local disabled people conducting the study and some of the problems they encountered. (Go to Activity Box 4.)

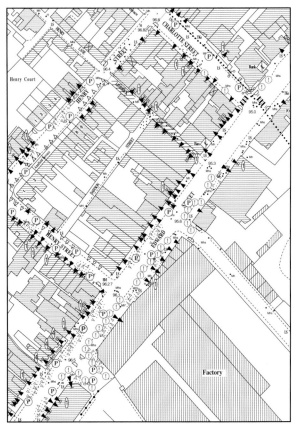

Figure 3: An extract of an accessibility map of Newbridge, Ireland, produced using the symbols shown in Information Box 4.

Activity Box 4: Making an accessibility map

Using the information you collected as part of Activity Box 2, create an accessibility map of your local shopping centre. Try to make the map as inclusive as possible so that it contains information suitable for people with different disabilities (e.g. wheelchair user, reduced mobility, visually impaired). One strategy may be to create maps dedicated to one particular group and then to merge them. Text should be in plain English and accompanied by visual logos (you may need to invent some) so that someone with a learning disability can understand the labelling.

Make sure you include details about the three parts of access: getting there, getting between the buildings and moving about inside the buildings.

The map should communicate issues of accessibility as clearly as possible, so take note of the following:

- Provide a reference and a title for your map (e.g. Accessibility map of Metro Centre Shopping Centre).
- Display at an appropriate size so that visual interpretation is easy and text readable.
- Make sure the map is uncluttered and contains the necessary information at an appropriate scale.
- Include a legend, scale and north arrow.

See Information Box 4 for examples of possible map symbols.
See Information Box 8 (page 40) and Activity Box 2 (page 13) for details of undertaking an access audit.

Tip: Remember that disabled people consist of more than just wheelchair users!

Information Box 4: Map symbols

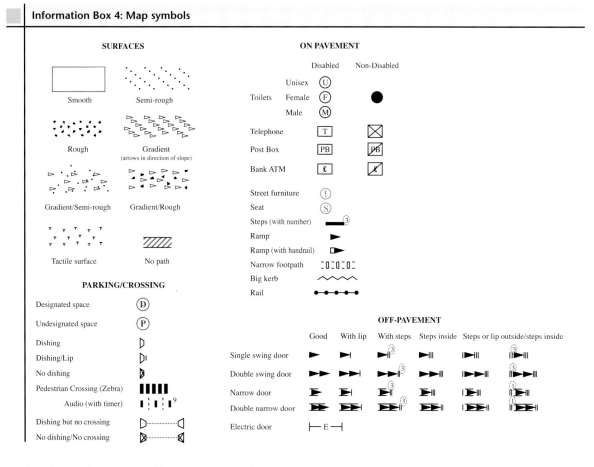

Another method adopted by some geographers to study access to the built environment is to examine how government policy and legislation shapes the urban landscape. The legislative framework in most Western countries has changed in recent years, with the introduction of legislation relating to disabled access to public spaces. In the UK, access to the built environment and to public space is covered by the Town and Country Planning Act 1990, Disabled Persons Act 1981, Part M of the Building Regulations 1985, 1992 and 1998, and the Disability Discrimination Act 1995. However, these pieces of legislation are weak, and as Imrie documents (1996, p. 135), are poorly enforced by some local authorities. For example, in his analysis of local authority enforcement of Building Regulations, Imrie found one authority where the Building Regulations were enforced only very sparingly, in just one-third of all cases. Of this third, less than 25 per cent of applications for planning permission conformed to the

Regulations, and the remaining 75 per cent were not penalised for failing to do so. Imrie also found that many authorities had great difficulty enforcing the Regulations, with developers choosing to ignore threats of action (which rarely materialised). Twenty-five per cent of authorities admitted that they had taken little or no action to enforce Part M. So while a mechanism for change is available, there is much resistance on the ground by both developers and authorities. This is not to say that improvements are not occurring, but that these improvements are slow to materialise.

Rob Imrie (1996) argues that the regulations are ineffective because their language is open to interpretation and because they apply only to certain buildings (i.e. new public buildings), excluding, for example, old buildings which might otherwise be adapted. However, by 2004 all buildings that provide a public service must have been adapted for disabled access. At present Building Regulations require 'reasonable provision' of access for disabled people (to help overcome ambiguities and update best practice, the Building Regulations and Standards are currently under review). But what is reasonable provision? Is it that all buildings should be fully accessible, or simply that they should have a ramp at the entrance? Is one accessible seating area in a cinema reasonable provision? The failure of planners and builders to interpret the use of 'reasonable provision' clauses in a positive light has recently led the Irish government to review its legislation, which is very similar to that in the UK. For example, the Minister for the Department of the Environment and Local Government (DoELG) recently published a document condemning those that have used the 'reasonable provision' clause to justify minimum access provision (DoELG, 1999). Disability groups have similarly criticised both the

law, and planners, and builders, interpretation of it, in the UK.

In order to place UK policy and law in a wider context, Imrie and others have examined legislation from a number of different countries. What they found is that the UK is lagging behind some countries in its access provision. For example, the 1990 Americans with Disabilities Act (ADA) provides comprehensive legislation that makes it illegal for any public building to be inaccessible to disabled people. Owners of property which fails to meet the ADA requirements are legally bound to improve the access to their buildings. What the US and other examples show is that the ways in which geography disables people differs between countries. They also provide useful guides as to how access might change and how this could be achieved.

Case study 2: Access to public transport

Access to public transport is vital to disabled people, especially since they generally have lower incomes than their non-disabled counterparts (see Case study 4, pages 24-26) and therefore cannot afford a car. Dependence on public transport in itself restricts freedom of movement, but when that transport is also unsuitable for disabled people, it presents a serious barrier. 'Unsuitability' includes poor design as well as inadequate provision (e.g. infrequent or unreliable services). Often journeys have to be planned several days in advance, to allow time to book provision. For example, it is not possible for wheelchair users to travel on the London Underground without booking 24 hours in advance, and even then travel is restricted to stations with a lift. Moreover, disabled people often have to travel circuitous routes and are denied the same choice of routes as non-disabled people. However, the situation is changing in some cities, as, for example, old buses are replaced by 'kneeling' buses, and more taxis become wheelchair friendly (Figure 4). Overall, the rate of change in the UK is slow and patchy, with some cities still placing orders for new, inaccessible buses.

Figure 4: Different modes of accessible and inaccessible transport. Photos: Department of Planning, Birmingham City Council, Sheila Gray/Format and Maggie Murray/Format.

Activity Box 5: Disability and public transport

1. Keep a weekly diary of where you go and how you get there.
2. For each trip document how easy it would be for (1) a wheelchair user, (2) a person using crutches, and/or (3) a blind person, to undertake the same trips. Note which, if any, of the modes of transport had been adapted for use by disabled people. Look for features/problems such as those in the photographs in Figure 4.
3. Using the information gathered from the above, critically appraise transport provision in your local area. If you think the situation could be improved, detail what improvements are needed and how they will help disabled people.
4. Write to the service provider with your findings.

One consequence for disabled people of unsuitable public transport is restricted access to employment and social events. Thus, it perpetuates unemployment and under-employment among disabled people which, in turn, restricts their ability to earn a living and means they tend to be confined to poor, cheap, and often inadequate housing and to become dependent on welfare. Given these far-reaching consequences it is therefore important to record public transport provision and to note how it affects disabled peoples' lives. (Go to Activity Box 5.)

Case study 3: Geographies of blindness

Of all the sensory and physical impairments, severe visual impairment has probably received the most attention from geographers. Vision is often quoted as the spatial sense *par excellence* and is thought to be central to an understanding of the geographic world. It is generally acknowledged that sight is vital for 'trouble-free' locomotion because it allows people to note the location of objects relative to themselves and to other objects. People with no or limited vision have to rely on using tactile (touch), proprioceptive (muscle position) and auditory (sound) senses to construct and understand the geography around them. As a result of his research findings, Reg Golledge (1993) argues that after communicating by reading and writing, the inability to travel independently and to interact with the wider world are the most significant problems resulting from visual impairment or blindness.

Most of the research relating to the geography of blindness has focused on how people with visual impairment process, learn and store the spatial information that they have gained. This can be through both primary interaction (e.g. walking about) and secondary sources (e.g. tactile maps), and on the viability and success of different mediums in communicating spatial information (see Chapter 5, pages 39-43). A less explored subject is the spatial experiences of people with severe visual impairments. This was the focus of a large-scale project comparing the spatial knowledge and experience of people with severe visual impairments living in Belfast, Northern Ireland, and Santa Barbara, California (Kitchin *et al.*, 1998a). Here, we will concentrate on the responses from people living in Belfast.

While all of the respondents in the study successfully, and in the main independently, travelled around Belfast during the course of their daily lives, every one of them had encountered difficulties. Following a detailed analysis of the interview transcripts it became clear that the problems encountered and the spatial confusion these induced (e.g. being lost or disorientated) could be divided into two distinct types – self-produced confusion and situational confusion. Self-produced confusion is spatial confusion caused through the actions or miscognition (incorrect thinking) of the visually impaired person as they navigate a route. Examples include attempting shortcuts and miscounting key choice points. (Key choice points are locations along a route, e.g. landmarks or turns that help people navigate.) In these cases, the visually impaired person is directly responsible for their spatial confusion, although their predicament may be made worse by situational confusion (confusion caused by a temporary or permanent localised occurrence). In this case, the person's confusion over their location, orientation and route, is caused by specific features and occurrences in the environment. Examples include roadworks, vehicles parked on the pavement, and street furniture (e.g. benches, bins and bollards) which all disrupt the paths taken by visually impaired people and require adjustment actions. A survey of young, blind people in the UK revealed that in the preceding week 20 per cent of respondents had not left their home; 34 per cent had travelled locally and only 41 per cent had left the confines of the home alone and on foot (Clark-Carter *et al.*, 1986). Other studies have found that that at least 30 per cent of people with severe visual impairments make no

independent journeys outside their homes. Among their reasons for a reluctance to leave the home, the young blind people frequently said the reason was 'situational confusion' caused by such things as disrupted pathways.

Information Box 5 provides examples of situational confusion and Information Box 6 the potential solutions that the visually impaired people suggested. When studying these quotes remember that only very few people who are registered as blind have no vision at all, most have some form of residual vision (Figure 5). (Go to Activity Box 6.)

Figure 5: Different types of visual impairment: (a) Combined central and peripheral vision loss (i.e. diabetic retinopathy), (b) peripheral field loss (i.e. glaucoma), (c) central field loss (i.e. macular degeneration), and (d) reduced contrast (i.e. cataract).
Photos: © Sign Design Guide 2000, courtesy of JMU Access Partnership.
Note: These images are meant as representations. Two-dimensional images can only give an impression of a sight condition. Particular conditions also vary according to the individual, the particular stage of an impairment and also environmental factors such as varying light conditions.

Information Box 5: Situational confusion encountered by visually impaired people

- 'A lot of shops now have huge amounts of pavement clutter ... if it is bright and there are lots of people then I will bump into things.'
- 'The cane is good, but there are things that it can't detect like head-high signs and skips which can do a lot of damage.'
- 'Here the streets are really narrow, and so are the footpaths. But they still have steps on to the pavement, jutting out, so it actually narrows the footpath in half again. There are also an awful lot of obstacles ... When they put trees in and take a tile out of the pavement it becomes a problem for me. They have flower boxes hanging off walls too, at head height, at body height.'
- 'Bin men leave the wheelie bins all over the place.'
- 'Prams and bicycles can be a real problem ... cars parked on pavements are a nuisance.'
- 'The cane doesn't detect overhangs. Last November a truck was parked at the side of the road. I came underneath it and whacked into the tailgate. I broke my nose and had two black eyes.'
- 'Some places in the shopping centres you have to go up and grope the shop front looking for the door. You don't know if it is a window or a door.'
- 'I try and avoid Castle Court [a shopping mall], everybody in it is all over the place [as opposed to ordinary shopping streets where people tend to walk in parallel lines along the pavement].'
- 'I was on the Antrim Road, lines of shops, traffic and there was CableTel digging holes. There were pneumatic drills going, it was really disorientating – I couldn't use the traffic noise to work out which way I was facing.'
- 'The only thing is, sometimes there isn't a pelican crossing, and there isn't a bleeper because of traffic management or whatever ... I find it frustrating. Half of me thinks the motorist is probably waving me across, but then I can't see him, so he's probably getting frustrated.'
- 'If I am on a train or a bus and it is a journey I've not done very often, I can be very anxious because it is travelling so quickly that until we get to the stops I can't possibly know where I am ... I have to concentrate really hard.'

Source: Kitchin *et al.*, 1998a, pp. 38-39.

Information Box 6: Potential solutions to situational confusion suggested by people with severe visual impairments

- 'Very simple practical ideas are needed, such as larger signs and painting the edges of all steps.'
- 'Larger signs are needed. Street signs in most towns are either too high or too low to read.'
- 'They should paint the kerbs, that would help. Sometimes I fall off even with the cane. I've been knocked down twice ... Drivers don't realise even if you have a cane. They don't really care. It scared me a bit last time, I just lost the edge of the kerb.'
- 'Move lamp posts to one side of the pavement.'
- 'Painting a shop doorway would be good, like a yellow line by the door. I'm always walking into shop fronts looking for the door.'
- 'Tactile pavements need to be standardised and there need to be more of them.'
- 'We need consistency, they are not uniform. You can spot a white line on one set of steps and then take a tumble on the next. Positioning of signs needs to be better.'
- 'We need consistency in tactile markings at crossings and road junctions. They are good in some areas but they don't always end up at the pole with the button ... If there was consistency it would really improve my confidence no end. Some go from the edge of the pavement to the inner shoreline, others just jut out into the path, so sometimes you can miss them.'

Source: Kitchin *et al.*, 1998a, p. 43.

Activity Box 6: Exploring geographies of blindness

Read through Information Boxes 5 and 6 then consider the following:

1. What sorts of problems do visually impaired people encounter on a daily basis?
2. Are the sorts of changes required by people with severe visual impairments difficult to implement? Give reasons.
3. Can you think of any other strategies that might help visually impaired people to move around easily?

Divide into pairs. One of you put on a blindfold and try and walk from one end of the school to the other. The other person should walk next to their blindfolded partner and stop them from coming to harm. Once at the other end, swap roles with the blindfolded person leading the way back to the start.

Now answer the following questions:

1. Was it easy to find your way?
2. What sorts of problems did you encounter that were difficult to negotiate or which made you confused?
3. How could the trip have been made easier (other than taking the blindfold off!)?

In groups of four or five construct a tactile accessibility map for a different part of the school (see Activity Box 4, page 18). The map should detail the layout of the buildings, rooms within the buildings and where the main obstacles and hazards are located. Use household items (textiles, plastics, foodstuffs) to create the map (remember it is not important how the map looks but how it feels). Include a legend and a scale.

Once complete compare maps and discuss their relative merits and limitations as a whole class.

You could work in pairs to evaluate another group's map, with one of you wearing a blindfold and trying to use the map to find his or her way about, and the other taking notes.

Case study 4: Access to employment

Geography has important implications for disabled people's access to the labour market. For example, if the work environment is inaccessible (e.g. has no disabled toilet, or has stairs but no ramp or lift) then disabled people will find it very difficult to work there. Similarly, if public transport to the workplace is inaccessible to disabled people, they will be excluded from finding employment there. Limited access to the workplace restricts disabled people's income which in turn restricts their spatial behaviour as they cannot afford to travel and go to social events.

The unemployment rate for disabled people is much higher than non-disabled people. In Ireland, the Irish Wheelchair Association (1994) found that 85 per cent of its members were unemployed. In the UK, while on average 8 per cent of non-disabled people remain unemployed over a two-year period, 26 per cent of disabled people remain jobless over the same time frame (Labour Force Survey, 1992). Where disabled people do gain access to the workplace it is often in manual, low-skilled occupations and they are relatively underpaid (Figure 6). For example, a UK Office of Census and Population Surveys (OCPS) conducted in the mid-1980s found that only 18 per cent of disabled men had managerial or professional jobs compared with 28 per cent for non-disabled men (Martin et al., 1989). Moreover, disabled people are more likely to be employed through informal arrangements that are not covered by formal contracts and employment legislation, thus leaving them more vulnerable.

The social and economic consequences of this exclusion are three-fold. First, disabled people are being denied the right to work and support themselves. This means that 50 per cent of disabled people and their families live below the basic standard of living. They are also denied the social experience of work and its attached social status. Disabled people are thus left isolated and bored, with reduced self-confidence and self-respect. Second, there are extra living costs for disabled people which have to be met either by the individual or the State. Despite some concessions many disabled people have to buy costly equipment such as wheelchairs, have their houses adapted for everyday living (such as fitting a downstairs bathroom) and have to pay increased costs for mandatory items such as car insurance. As such, the OCPS (Martin et al., 1989) estimated that in 1988 essential extra living costs for disabled people were on average £20.00 a week more than non-disabled people. The Disablement Income Group (Thompson *et al.*, 1990) thought this to be a large underestimation and suggested it was nearer £100. Berthoud *et al.* (1993), suggest £50.00 for severe disablement and £40.00 for mid-disablement[2]. Third, social security payments to support unemployed disabled people are expensive to the State and yet in many cases are not adequate to maintain the basic, minimum standard of living. This limits spatial and social behaviour. (Go to Activity Box 7.)

Two national skills schemes, 'AbilityNet' (set up in the 1980s) and 'Workability' (set up by Leonard Cheshire in 1998), have been helping disabled people overcome problems in the workplace. In addition, the Disability Rights Commission launched in April 2000 will put pressure on employers to adapt working environments to meet the needs of disabled people (see websites, page 48).

Activity Box 7: Access to employment

Examine the following quotes taken from a study of access to employment in Donegal, in the west of Ireland.

- 'How is anybody supposed to live on £70 a week? In my case I'm living on my own and I've a house to keep, fuel to buy, electricity to pay, telephone to pay and how are you supposed to pay out of that? If it's £70 then it's ten pounds a day to live on ... And this is where I was talking about the hidden costs of disability. They don't take into account that if we want to go somewhere and you haven't got a car of your own you need to pay for a taxi.'
- 'There are no buses. Unless I take a taxi I can't go anywhere, and I can't afford a taxi.'
- 'I think the biggest single problem not only amongst disability but all the other different organisations is transport. We just have no transport. So, you create a job tomorrow in Letterkenny but there's just no transport to get you there.'
- 'I'm a qualified legal executive. But I can't get any work because of access, because I am a wheelchair user. The majority of the courts are inaccessible, where I would be spending a lot of my time. And most of the solicitor's offices.'
- 'I lost faith with the whole process. I didn't see the point because you just meet the same old problems. That's what happens. You don't get the job because you are disabled.'
- 'I mean I never received no careers advice when I was at school.'
- 'I don't think there's any careers, certainly not for disabled people. The only thing they will do is say "you may be eligible for this scheme why don't you go and do that?" ... There's no jobs.'
- 'It's like they've been forgotten like, this training scheme ends and another one begins. People spend years and never get a job. And the scheme changes each year and might not have any relevance to the scheme the previous year.'
- 'You also have people going on training schemes they have no interest in – they only went on it because someone told them to. We're that conditioned over the years to do what we are told that when someone tells you to go and do a course – you go and do it. You may have no interest. Government bodies tell you that "we know what's best for you".'
- 'Well I was there recently at some training, with small employers, and they were amazed themselves that disabled people were capable of doing as much as they were. Because they didn't think they could, through ignorance, through non-awareness.'

Source: Kitchin *et al.*, 1998b, pp. 792-9.

Answer the following questions:

1. What do the quotes reveal about the sorts of geographical factors that hinder disabled people's access to employment?
2. What are the consequences of these factors to the everyday lives of disabled people?
3. How do you think that access to employment might be improved for disabled people?

---

2. There is significant inflation on these figures as they are 10 years old.

Figure 6: Disabled people in the workplace. Photos: Joanne O'Brien/Format and Sally Lancaster/Format.

Case study 5: Segregated schooling

Segregated education can be traced back to the late eighteenth century when institutions were established in France (deaf, 1760; blind, 1784; retarded, 1798), in Scotland (deaf and dumb, 1760) and in England (blind, 1791). In other Western European countries, segregated education grew out of the institutionalisation of disabled people in asylums and poorhouses throughout the nineteenth century. Schools were often started by voluntary organisations but later came under State control (e.g. the Elementary Schools Act of 1893 in England and Wales required local authorities to provide segregated schooling). Many of them were residential schools and so were often some distance away from people's home base. As such, the schooling of disabled children in separate geographic locations has a long history. Those who controlled the education system argued that segregation made sense for the following reasons:

- **Economically** – specialised resources were more economically viable if concentrated because the numbers of disabled children are generally small (typically 3-5 per cent of children).
- **Academically** – segregating disabled students meant that those in ordinary schools were not held back through placing too many demands on teachers and resources.
- **Socially** – the eugenics movement (disabled people should be eradicated) in the West was just starting (i.e. late nineteenth/early twentieth century) at the time of most special education schools and many believed that keeping 'defective' and 'ordinary' children apart was a sensible strategy.
- **Morally** – it 'protected' disabled children, who were viewed as unable to cope with the wider world, within a humanitarian environment.

This means that disabled children have to attend school outside their local community, often having to travel relatively long distances to attend, and in the case of some schools children are boarders (in deaf schools in Ireland, for example, where children board from the age of five). In other words, disabled children often live in different geographic spheres from other children in their community (see Activity Box 8). As described on page 17, this has a number of negative effects upon the lives of disabled children, such as:

- it does not prepare children well for life beyond school,
- it provides a narrow range of educational opportunities,
- it separates children from their peers both socially and geographically,
- it reinforces attitudes that disabled people are different (this is a key one to disabled people themselves), and

- it channels resources that need to be spread between children who have a range of abilities (up to 20 per cent of children need some level of remedial teaching).

This is not to deny that some disabled children need specialised teaching provision, and many receive this. However, children of all abilities can share the same school space, the classroom and dining room, if not the same playground (Figure 7).

Figure 7:
Inclusive play time.
Photo: Paula
Solloway/Format.

Activity Box 8: Access to education

In a recent study of access to mainstream schools for disabled children in County Kildare, Ireland, Kitchin and Mulcahy (1999) found that:

- 0.41 per cent of children had physical or sensory impairments
- 55 per cent of first-level (age 5-11) and 71.4 per cent of second-level schools (age 11-18) considered themselves to be physically accessible to disabled children.
- 40 per cent of first-level and 50 per cent of second-level schools considered themselves to be educationally accessible to disabled children

Study Tables 2 and 3.
1. What do the Tables reveal about access to education for disabled children?
2. Do the Tables support the above statements in relation to how accessible the schools thought they were?
3. What are the consequences of inaccessible schools to disabled children?
4. How accessible is your own school/college, and what does this mean to local disabled students?

Table 2: Access provision in Kildare schools

Provision	First-level (age 5-11)			Second-level (age 11-18)		
	Yes (%)	No (%)	Don't know/ not applicable/ no answer (%)	Yes (%)	No (%)	Don't know/ not applicable/ no answer (%)
Parking spaces	61.6	30	8.3	85.7	7.1	7.1
Accessible staffroom	45	45	10	64.3	14.3	21.4
Accessible classrooms	45	45	10	64.3	14.3	21.4
Low counters/desks	35	51.6	13.3	14.3	57.1	28.6
Ramp and stairs at main entrance	31.6	61.6	6.6	42.8	28.6	28.6
Other accessible entrance	20	58.3	38.3	35.7	7.1	57.1
Accessible sports facilities	28.3	60	11.6	42.8	21.4	35.7
Accessible toilet	26.6	66.6	6.6	71.4	7.1	21.4
Colour-contrasted walls	10	75	15	7.1	64.3	28.6
Large-print signs	8.3	75	16.6	21.4	50	28.6
Tactile floorways	5	65	30	7.1	35.7	57.1
Accessible lift	0	66.6	33.3	7.1	28.6	64.3
Automatic door	0	75	25	0	50	50
Minicom/induction loop	0	90	10	0	71.4	28.6
Access rooms plus Minicom	0	65	35	0	42.8	57.1

Table 3: Access to educational support/resources in Kildare schools

Provision	First-level (age 5-11)			Second-level (age 11-18)		
	Yes (%)	No (%)	Don't know/ not applicable/ no answer (%)	Yes (%)	No (%)	Don't know/ not applicable/ no answer (%)
Remedial teaching	91.6	8.3	0	71.4	28.6	0
Computer (PC)	83.3	3.3	16.6	92.9	0	7.1
Library	81.6	15	3.3	71.4	28.6	0
Computer disk	38.3	38.3	23.3	21.4	42.8	35.7
Adapted PC/software (learning)	25	61.6	13.3	14.3	78.6	7.1
Tape	23.3	66.6	20	7.1	50	42.8
Large print	21.6	53.3	25	7.1	64.3	28.6
Compact disk	16.6	73.3	26.6	14.3	42.8	42.8
Adapted PC/software (physical)	3.3	83.3	13.3	0	92.9	7.1
Specialised equipment	1.6	88.3	10	21.4	64.3	7.1
Adapted PC/software (sight)	1.6	85	13.3	7.1	85.7	7.1
Braille	0	76.6	23.3	0	57.1	42.8

Case study 6: Institutions

In order to understand the social position of disabled people in today's society we need to refer back in time to different periods of our history. One historical geographer who has done this is Chris Philo (1987). He has sought to understand the development and geography of asylums, charitable lunatic hospitals and private 'madhouses' in nineteenth century Britain by analysing the articles and editorials contained within the *Asylum Journal*, a journal concerning mental health institutions and practice. His work highlights how geography was organised to separate people with mental impairments or mentally ill people from the rest of society (Figure 8). Thinking at that time was dominated by a set of ideas that promoted segregated institutions sited in tranquil and rural environments. These sites not only segregated 'patients', placing them out of sight and mind of the general population, but were thought to offer suitable environments for treatment and recovery because they were away from the distractions of home and urban life, and in airy and spacious surroundings. Philo observes that, in many cases, great care was taken to analyse such things as climate, soil, underlying rock type, topography, elevation, aspect and even vegetation cover, as all were thought to be important for creating a 'healthy mind'. Such was the power of this set of ideas that it is only in the last two decades that the role of asylums and residential nursing homes has been questioned and ideas concerning independent and sheltered living, and community care, put firmly on the agenda. (Go to Activity Box 9.)

Figure 8: People with mental illnesses were often separated from society into long-term psychiatric units. Photo: Paula Glassman/Format.

Activity Box 9: Thinking about institutional care homes

Examine the following statement by Chris Philo:

'There is nothing "natural" about removing the mentally distressed from the normal round of people and places in a society, or then placing them apart in houses designed to serve the various purposes of restraint, shelter and treatment. Rather, whenever and wherever it has occurred, this process of separation – which is both social and spatial – has been informed by quite specific social, cultural and professional understandings of "madness"' (Philo, 1987, pp. 401-2).

Then think about and answer the following questions:

1. Do you think that having a system of institutional care homes is the best way to cater for people who have developmental or psychiatric disabilities or who are considered mentally ill? Justify your answer.
2. To what extent do you agree with Philo's assertion that 'there is nothing "natural" about removing the mentally distressed from the normal round of people and places in a society'?
3. How would you go about creating an inclusive society in which people with developmental and psychiatric disabilities and people who are mentally ill are a part?

Discuss your answers as a class.

Case study 7: Resisting disabling geographies

So far we have examined the ways in which disabled people are disabled by geographical factors. These factors, however, are not unconditionally accepted by disabled people, who themselves use geography to resist disabling environments. Disabled people have always resisted the non-disabled opinions and practices that affect them, but mainly in ways that are defiant and individual based. Traditionally, the action taken has included living the lives they want, getting an education and a job, having children, not hiding their 'deformities', rejecting certain treatments, battling against stereotypes and prejudice, and seeking acceptance from non-disabled people. In recent decades, however, disabled people and their allies have started to explore collective and more confrontational ways to challenge disabling practices.

In the early 1970s a disabled equal opportunities movement began to grow in Britain. Disabled activists started to take over organisations that claimed to represent them or set up their own organisations such as the Union of Physically Impaired Against Segregation (UPIAS). In more recent years, advocacy groups such as Disabled People's Direct Action Network (DAN) have used direct protest and civil disobedience to highlight disability issues (see Figure 9).

Direct protest, while rare, is interesting to look at because it uses a strategy of disrupting geography – of bringing to a stop or disrupting the activities that ordinarily take place in a given location. For example, in 1995 DAN protested outside the Houses of Parliament about the failure of the then Conservative government to pass the Civil Rights (Disabled Persons) Bill. This site was chosen by DAN for two reasons. First, the attention of MPs would be drawn to disabling practices. Second, the protest was guaranteed to draw much needed media attention to the need for a comprehensive civil rights bill and to keep up the pressure on the government. By crawling up the steps of Parliament and chaining themselves to buses, members of DAN vividly demonstrated the problems of inaccessibility that they face, and therefore the need for new legislation. DAN's actions were timed to coincide with parliamentary debates concerning the Bill and the protest was carefully stage-managed in space and time to try and make the maximum impact. In 1996, DAN extended its political campaigning to include demonstrations within key marginal seats, and especially those whose MP had failed to address disability issues, in the lead-up to the 1997 general election. DAN's strategy of focusing on particular locations was intended to change the political map and to bring about the downfall of the governing political party. These political protests, and other actions such as handcuffing themselves to buses and trains, were intended to show the 'geography' that disabled people experience everyday.
(Go to Activity Box 10.)

Activity Box 10: Thinking about disabled people's resistance

Answer the following questions in relation to the two newspaper extracts shown in Figure 9.

1. What did the protesters do?
2. Was geography important in their strategy?
3. Was the media sympathetic to their cause?
4. Was the protest a success – did the protesters get what they wanted?

If you are, or were, disabled answer the following questions:

1. What sorts of things would you want to demonstrate about?
2. How would you go about making yourself heard by people who have the power to change things?

Discuss the answers to these questions as a class.

Write a short newspaper report (500 words) detailing provision for disabled people in your local town. Note both good and bad aspects, and suggest how direct action might change the situation.

Disabled protesters handcuffed to train

(Peter Thacker, writing in the Yorkshire Evening Post, 25 October 1996)

Rail passengers were stranded this morning when several disabled protesters chained themselves to a train. Six members of the Disabled Peoples' Direct Action Network, most of whom were in wheelchairs, handcuffed themselves to a train leaving New Pudsey Station. They were protesting about the lack of disabled facilities on public transport.

The 8.14am Leeds to Manchester train was delayed for more than an hour while police negotiated with about 40 demonstrators in an attempt to get them to call off their action.

Eventually British Transport Police arrived with bolt cutters to physically remove the protesters, who had travelled from all over the North.

David Colley, from Newcastle, was among those who handcuffed himself to the train. He said, 'In order to get noticed we have got to do something like this. Up to now we have been ignored. All we want is access to public transport like everybody else.'

Leeds protester Jill Morris said: 'We don't want to do something like this but it has been forced on us. We want full accessibility to public transport for everyone. In the short term we would like talks with Metro to find out exactly what they are doing.'

Darryl McManus, 26, from Morley, was one of about 50 commuters delayed by the protest. He said 'It's a rather extreme measure but I suppose I can understand it.'

No one was available for comment at Metro.

Protest crawl over rights for disabled

(Steve Boggan, writing in The Independent, 24 May 1994)

'Piss on pity' said the tee-shirts and the wheelchair logos, but it was indeed a pitiful sight; half a dozen disabled people crawling on their hands and knees, begging for access to the Mother of Parliament.

Tourists were halted yesterday at the sight of the group, some being wheeled, others being dragged or dragging themselves from one gate to another to protest against the skulduggery that stymied the Bill that would have guaranteed their civil rights.

The protest at the Palace of Westminster was organised by the Disabled People's Direct Action Network in the wake of the admission by Nicholas Scott, Minister for the Disabled, that his department drafted the 80-odd amendments that led to the Civil Rights (Disabled Persons) Bill being talked out of Parliament.

Yesterday's protest was intended to be symbolic – the group wanted to crawl into the St Stephen's entrance of the Palace of Westminster – but it became real when they were denied access for five hours.

Despite being invited in by Dennis Skinner, Labour MP for Bolsover, six people who abandoned their wheelchairs were refused access by Philip Wright, a deputy Serjeant at Arms, who said that St Stephen's entrance was unsuitable as it has 14 steps.

After being promised access at the Carriage Gate, the main entrance for MPs in cars, the group began their 100-metre crawl. It took 53 minutes of tearing trousers and scuffing shoes.

They had to wait for a further three hours. Even when two asked to go to the toilet, they were directed to a public convenience 200 metres away. Finally, after the intervention of Mr Skinner in the House, the Speaker, Betty Boothroyd, said the party should be given access and they were wheeled in to lobby their MPs.

Figure 9: Extracts on DAN protests from a national and a local newspaper.
Reproduced with the permission of *The Independent* and *Yorkshire Post Newspapers*.

CHAPTER 4

UNDERSTANDING WHY GEOGRAPHY DISABLES

To understand why a geography which disables people exists, we need to consider how society operates to exclude some groups of people. Disabled people are not the only group to be discriminated against in Western society. Table 4 lists seven forms of discrimination and shows who, in general, are the oppressors (agents) and the victims (targets). You probably belong to a mix of agent and target groups. Here, it is important to remember that while in general disabled people in Western society are more discriminated against than non-disabled people, most live full and fulfilling lives, but lives that are constrained in various ways, e.g. by reduced access. Moreover, in some cases agent and targets are reversed, depending on the context. For example, a disabled person might bully a non-disabled person or behave in a racist way. When reading through the rest of this chapter try to think about your position as both agent and target, and what it would be like to be disabled. To give this context, try playing the games in Activity Box 11 and then answer the questions in Activity Box 12.

Activity Box 11: Exclusion games

Try playing the following games in your group or class.

Game 1

Materials: A set of cards made from green, blue and red paper, roughly 10cm x 6cm in size. The number of cards you make will depend on how many take part.

On each green card write one of the following orders, or other orders you make up yourselves: 'Hop on one leg', 'Clean the blackboard', 'Stack the chairs', 'Open the window', 'Make animal noises', 'Count backwards from 100', 'Sing a song'.

On each blue and red card write 'You must do whatever the Greens tell you'.

1. Divide the class randomly into Green, Red and Blue groups and distribute the cards among them. The Green group has all the power and Red and Blue members have to do as asked.
2. The Green group sits down. They tell the members of the Red group to stand facing the wall with their noses touching the wall, to remain silent and to not look round. The Blue group has to perform all the activities written on the cards, as dictated by the Green group.
3. Let the game run for 10 minutes then discuss what happened and how members of the Green (power) group, Blue (controlled) group and Red (excluded/powerless) group felt.

Game 2

Materials: Packet of dried peas (or marbles or similar), blindfolds and material to tie hands and feet.

1. Clear the room of obstacles (move desks to edges). Divide the class into four groups.
2. Group 1 have their hands tied together. Group 2 have their feet tied together. Group 3 are blindfolded. Group 4 are left as they are.
3. Empty the peas onto the floor. Each group, on the command of 'go', must try to collect as many peas as possible (within safety limits). The group who collects the most peas within a given time limit wins.
4. Discuss how members of each group felt while playing the game and how fair they felt the game was. Try and make connections with how members of different 'excluded' groups feel (e.g. disabled people, homeless people) and how they are excluded.

Adapted from: Gill and Loughman, no date, p. 21.

Activity Box 12: Thinking about exclusion

Before reading the rest of this chapter, think through and answer the following questions:

1. Why are disabled people not treated by society in the same way as non-disabled people?
2. Why do some people feel anxious, nervous or fear in the company of disabled individuals?
3. Why do many people fear becoming disabled?

Produce a list summarising how people in the class answered each question. Discuss each list. Discuss how would you feel about the answers if you were disabled.

Ableism

As shown in Table 4, discrimination against disabled people because of their impairment is called *ableism*. Disabled people are discriminated against in all sorts of ways, and many types of ableism can be identified (see Information Box 7). Iris Marion Young (1990) suggests that the discrimination expressed as ablesim, as with other forms of oppression such as racism, can be divided into five general types:

1. *Disabled people are rendered 'powerless'*: disabled people are kept in the same social position through political means and by being denied access to important decision-making positions within society. Disabled people are generally under-represented in political positions at all levels (local, regional, national and international) and therefore lack a platform from which to present their views.
2. *Disabled people are marginalised within society and social life*: disabled people are kept in the same social position through social means. Disabled people are generally 'pushed' into poor housing, denied access to private and public transport, and find it difficult to take part in 'mainstream' social activities (such as visiting the pub or cinema) because of poor provision and weak statutory laws.
3. *Disabled people are exploited within the labour market*: disabled people are kept in the same social position through material means. Disabled people are often excluded from the labour market through discriminatory practices and poor levels of mobility. Where they do gain access it is usually in marginal positions undertaking low-paid, low-skilled work, often on a part-time basis. Such a situation works to deny disabled people prosperity and wealth, and the power associated with these.
4. *Some disabled people are suppressed through violent means*: some disabled people are controlled through physical violence and imprisonment. For example, placing some disabled people against their wishes in asylums and other institutions both confines and oppresses them.
5. *Disabled people are stigmatised through the use of cultural representations and myths*: non-disabled cultural practices, lifestyles and images are promoted as the norm and in general disabled people are portrayed as abnormal and 'freaks of nature', thus legitimating the oppressive behaviour of non-disabled people towards disabled people.

Table 4: Forms of oppression, oppressors and victims

Form of oppression	Agent group	Target group
Ableism	Non-disabled people	Disabled people
Ageism	Young and middle-aged adults	Young people, old people
Antisemitism	Gentiles, Christians	Jews
Classism	Owning class, upper-middle class	Lower-middle class, working class, underclass
Heterosexism	Heterosexuals	Lesbians, gay men, bisexuals, transsexuals
Racism	Whites	Blacks, Asians, bi-racial people
Sexism	Men	Women

Source: Hardiman and Jackson, 1997.

Information Box 7: Ableism – a glossary of terms

Ableism. The systematic discrimination against disabled people by non-disabled people through individual, institutional and social/cultural means.

Active ableism. Actions which have as their stated or explicit goal the maintenance of a system of ableism and the oppression of disabled people. An example is the active campaigning for asylums or the closure of care in the community schemes.

Ally. A non-disabled person who actively works to eliminate ableism. This person may be motivated by self-interest in ending ableism, a sense of moral obligation, or a commitment to foster social justice, as opposed to a patronising agenda of 'wanting to help those poor disabled people'.

Collusion. Thinking and acting in ways that support ableism.

Cultural ableism. Those aspects of society that overtly and covertly attribute value and normality to non-disabled people and devalue, stereotype and label disabled people as 'other'. An example is defining disability as abnormal and emphasising the achievements of those disabled people who try to 'overcome' their impairment.

Discrimination. The differential allocation of goods, resources and services, and the limitation of access to full participation in society based on individual membership of a particular social group.

Empowered disabled person. A disabled person who has an understanding of ableism and its impact on one's life without responding to events and circumstances as a victim.

Horizontal ableism. Is where disabled people themselves believe, act on and enforce the dominant non-disabled system of discrimination. Horizontal ableism can occur between members of the same group (a person with a spinal injury telling another to try harder to 'overcome' their impairment – enforcing the medical model of disability) or between different groups (a visually impaired person not wanting a psychiatric unit built near his or her home).

Individual ableism. The beliefs, attitudes and actions of individuals that perpetuate ableism. Individual ableism can be both consciously (deliberately) and subconsciously practised, and can be both active and passive in nature. An example is the telling of ableist jokes.

Institutional ableism. The network of institutional structures, policies, and practices that create advantages and benefits for non-disabled people, and discrimination, oppression and disadvantage for disabled people. An example is the prioritising of housing, education and employment strategies for non-disabled people.

Internalised ableism. Is where disabled people believe, act on and enforce the beliefs of the dominant non-disabled community. Examples include disabled people trying to become more 'normal', or believing that the best people to look after their interests are non-disabled people.

Non-disabled privilege. The concrete benefits of having access to resources, social rewards and power which non-disabled people receive by virtue of their health in an ableist society.

Passive ableism. Beliefs, attitudes and actions that contribute to the maintenance of ableism, without openly advocating the oppression of disabled people. An example would be staying silent when active ableism is being expressed.

Adapted from: Wejeyesinghe *et al.*, 1997, pp. 88-9, 93, 97-8.

These five forms of discrimination interlink to form a cycle of socialisation that works to reproduce discrimination (Figure 10).

Representations and myths

The first four of Young's points have been discussed earlier (pages 13-31), so here we concentrate on her last point – the stigmatisation of disabled people through the use of cultural representations and myths (Young, 1990). In these representations, target groups (in this case disabled people) are portrayed in a 'bad light', and the legitimacy of these representations sustained through myths. These representations take on a number of forms but often portray those who do not belong to the agent group as being impure, defiled, contaminated or dirty. As Len Barton has argued, 'labels such as "invalid", "cripple", "spastic", "handicapped" and "retarded" all imply both a functional loss and a lack of worth' (Barton, 1996, p. 8), and when used in reference to a non-disabled person it means that they are weak or stupid. The use of these terms perpetuates and legitimates offensive responses by non-disabled people including horror, fear, anxiety, hostility, distrust, pity, over-protection and patronising behaviour. As a consequence, disabled people are often viewed as 'freaks of nature', deemed to be abnormal, unproductive, unattractive, anti-social and tainted by

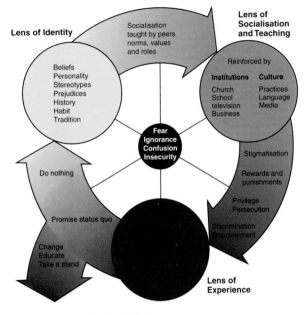

Figure 10: The cycle of socialisation

disease/ill-health. Such is the stigma of the disability label that many disabled people deny or seek to hide their impairment.

The media could do much to correct these negative images, but most media coverage is in the form not of positive images, but of pleas for charity contributions, seeking to invoke pity and sympathy,

---

Activity Box 13: Media portrayal of disabled people

Examine the following quote from Colin Barnes and then answer the questions below.

'Disabling stereotypes which medicalise, patronise, criminalise and dehumanise disabled people abound in books, films, on television, and in the press. They form the bedrock on which attitudes towards, assumptions about and the expectations of disabled people are based. They are fundamental to the discrimination and exploitation which disabled people encounter daily and contribute significantly to their systematic exclusion from mainstream community life' (Barnes, 1992, p. 39).

1. To what extent do you think the media shapes our attitudes towards disabled people?
2. In some Disney films, many of the 'baddies' are disabled or disfigured. Think of characters from other films, and in books and television, who are disabled. How are they represented?
3. Look through recent copies of a newspaper and detail how disabled people are represented. Pay particular attention to the type of language that is used and the feelings the articles arouse (see Figure 9, page 31).

As a class discuss your answers to the above questions.

Choose one of the photographs shown in Figure 11 and discuss the image it portrays.

Figure 11: Disability in the media: stills from (a) *My Left Foot* and (b) *The Hunchback of Notre Dame,* can be compared and contrasted with (c) an advertisement by *The Guardian* as well as the reaction of women in wheelchairs to the latter. Images: British Film Institute and Brenda Prince/Format.

and reinforcing the idea that disabled people cannot cope and need constant aid (see Activity Box 13). As organisations run by disabled people have recently been arguing, what disabled people want is full rights to housing, education and work; they do not want to not be reliant on charity. Media representations such as those described here might seem harmless but are powerful psychological tools that shape how we view other groups. Similarly, while an ableist joke might just seem like a bit of fun, it is in fact helping to sustain discriminatory ideas.

Myths on disability and sexuality

Closely related to cultural representations, myths take the form of malicious gossip which feeds into stereotypical representations (Figure 12). There are many myths relating to disabled people but here, for illustrative purposes, we will focus on one set only, namely myths relating to disability and sexuality. Our sexuality is an important part of our cultural identity – who we are. However, myths work to deny disabled people, both women and men, the freedom to express their sexual identity. It is often assumed, contrary to reality, that disabled people are asexual (i.e. lacking a biological sex drive), or are unable to partake in sexual activity, and that disabled people (particularly those with a developmental/intellectual disability) lack the requisite social judgement to behave sexually in a socially responsible manner. It is on the basis of this logic that many intellectually disabled women have been forcibly sterilised.

Among the common myths relating to disabled people and sexuality the following are typical:

Figure 12: Quasimodo's doomed adoration of Esmerelda is the focus for much of the story in *The Hunchback of Notre Dame*. Image: British Film Industry. Reproduced with permission of the BBC Photo Library.

- disabled people are asexual;
- disabled people who are not married do not have sex (and those who are married did so before they became disabled);
- disabled people cannot be parents; if a parent becomes disabled, his or her children are not getting a 'real' parent;
- in relationships, the non-disabled person runs the relationship;
- disabled people should be grateful for a sexual relationship;
- disabled people are too fragile for sexual activity;
- all disabled people are heterosexual.

People with disabilities are thus portrayed as having a poor body image and of being unable ever to fulfil their role in society. What follows from these assumptions is the perception of disabled people as economically unproductive and thus a burden to society. A consequence of these myths is that disabled women, for example, are less likely to have received sex education and certain health checks such as smear

tests and internal and breast examinations. In relation to men, whose identity is often defined around sexual prowess, fitness and work, there are also many myths which can seriously undermine their sense of masculinity.

Several researchers have noted that it is common for disabled people to suffer from low self-esteem and feelings of inferiority due to their disability and body image (Barton, 1996). The fact that the myths have gained common currency means that they may contribute to the breakdown of marriages and relationships when one partner becomes disabled or suffers chronic pain. In such cases, the healthy partner can place a strain on a relationship through a tendency to mother, infantilise (treat like children) and overprotect their disabled partner, or through behaviour changes due to a fear of hurting their partner or 'catching' a condition. It is not surprising, under such circumstances, that 75 per cent of women who become disabled are later divorced (although not always because of their disability) (Pitzele, 1995).

Activity Box 14: Geographies of disability and sexuality

Examine Figure 12 and the following two quotes and then answer the questions below

'... the disability rights movement has never addressed sexuality as a key political issue, though many of us find sexuality to be the area of our great oppression. We may well be more concerned with being loved and finding sexual fulfilment than getting on a bus' (Waxman and Finger, 1991, p. 1).

'There is an unspoken taboo about relationships and disabled people. Disabled people's sexual and emotional needs are rarely included in any discussion or representation in everyday life, whether this is in the newspapers and magazines we read, or the movies we watch. This reinforces the view of disabled people as "sick and sexless" rather than participating in full sexual and family relationships.' (Lamb and Layzell, 1994, p. 21).

1. Provide an interpretation of Figure 12. Do you think that it provides a good summary image of how disabled people's sexuality is conceived by non-disabled people? Justify your answer.
2. Think of disabled characters from films, books and television (see Figure 12), how many of them are in 'successful', loving relationships. Are many of them portrayed as 'sick and sexless'?
3. How comfortable would you be about:
   (a) Starting a personal relationship with a disabled partner?
   (b) Being with a partner who becomes disabled?
Explain your answers.

As a class discuss your answers to the above questions.

CHAPTER 5

TACKLING DISABLING GEOGRAPHY

As well as identifying how geography disables people, geographers can help to remove disabling barriers by offering advice and knowledge to policy makers and engineers concerning a range of practical issues.

Planning the built environment

If society is to become more inclusive and to respect disabled people for the abilities they have, and the people they are, then one essential requirement is to make the built environment more accessible. It was to achieve this end that the Disability Discrimination Act was passed in 1995, making it a legal obligation for service providers and employers in the UK to cater for the needs of disabled people. More recently the Disability Rights Commission was set up (in April 2000)

to monitor the effectiveness of disability legislation and fight discrimination against disabled people. It is because of their skills relating to mapping, surveying and people-centred research that geographers are able to help employers and others to meet their obligations. For example, geographers can identify particular problems and issues, and determine what structural changes in the environment are needed (see Information Box 8). While geographers can make significant progress on their own initiative, if the work is to be carried out successfully then disabled people need to be fully consulted since it is only they who can fully reveal the true extent of inaccessibility and potential solutions.

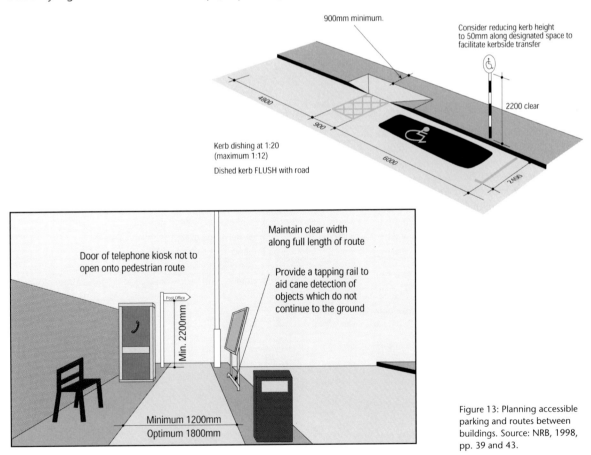

Figure 13: Planning accessible parking and routes between buildings. Source: NRB, 1998, pp. 39 and 43.

Information Box 8: Carrying out an access audit

One tangible action that geographers can take is to conduct an access audit of an environment to find out how accessible it is for disabled people. Central to the ideas of accessibility is the notion of 'universal accessibility' – designing for everyone. Many people who are not disabled can experience difficulty moving through an environment, such as mothers with small children, people carrying heavy/awkward loads, people who are temporarily injured.

In general, an access audit focuses on four major issues:

1. freedom of movement – independence/equal opportunity
2. ease of use/maintenance
3. improved functional efficiency
4. life safety provisions

To help you conduct an access audit, look at the checklist below (you could copy this for your own use). For each building, or the spaces between buildings, check that the condition is in place. You will need one audit form for each building (i.e. if there are 10 buildings you should complete 10 forms).

Specific issues to focus on:

Parking and approach (see Figure 13):
- ❏ well signposted and easy-to-find car park
- ❏ designated car spaces for disabled people that are close to the building
- ❏ trained staff available to help disabled people (with signs to indicate so)
- ❏ accessible path from car park to buildings (e.g. dropped kerbs)
- ❏ user-friendly path for people with sensory impairments (e.g. tactile paving)
- ❏ obstacles (e.g. bollards/street furniture) highlighted by colour contrast and tactile surfaces

Entrances to buildings (see Figure 14):
- ❏ provision of both steps and ramp
- ❏ hand-rails provided on both sides of steps/ramp
- ❏ doorbell can be reached by all
- ❏ audible/tactile/visible intercom
- ❏ easy-opening door
- ❏ level threshold across doorway
- ❏ door width sufficient to allow wheelchair access

Source: Ewart, 1998.

Reception and facilities:
- ❏ height of reception desk
- ❏ adequate seating
- ❏ publicly accessible toilets
- ❏ map of site including levels of accessibility

Circulation areas:
- ❏ adequate directional signage (tactile as well as visual)
- ❏ corridors wide enough
- ❏ level fire exits
- ❏ floor surface
- ❏ tactile paths/guides

Vertical circulation:
- ❏ lift large enough to accommodate wheelchair
- ❏ doors open wide enough
- ❏ height of control panel
- ❏ alarm/phone height
- ❏ audible and visible signage
- ❏ dimensions of treads/insets of stairs
- ❏ hand-rails to both sides of stairs and in contrasting colours
- ❏ stair nosing (edge of step) of a contrasting colour

Figure 14: Examples of accessible urban planning.
Photos: Birmingham City Council Department of Planning and Architecture.

Technical aids/maps

Another area in which geographers and cartographers are able to provide practical help to disabled people is in the development and testing of navigation aids for people with visual impairments, and by providing accessibility maps. The aids currently being developed to help people with visual impairments to navigate independently through the built environment can be divided into two groups: in-field and learning-based. In-field aids are designed to be used by the visually impaired person *in situ*, as they actually traverse an environment. The aids include talking signs (audible beacons sited in the environment which visually impaired people follow), personal guidance systems (which link satellite positioning technology with an electronic map to guide a person through an environment by giving directions), and tactile strip maps (maps that can be learnt through touch). Learning-based aids are designed to help visually impaired people learn how to traverse a route before they actually try to navigate through an environment. Examples include tactile maps (Figure 15), sound maps (maps which make different noises as features are touched), and talking maps (which give a list of directions) (Figure 16).

Reg Golledge, himself blind, has been using his skills as a geographer to help develop and test all of the in-field and learning-based orientation and

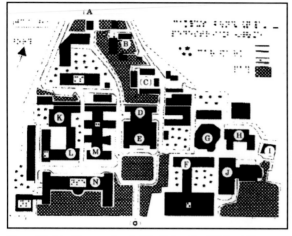

Figure 15: A tactile map of part of the University of Wales at Swansea campus.

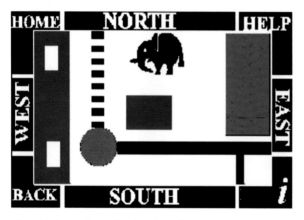

Figure 16: A sound map of an imaginary city.

mobility aids given as examples here. His research has shown that all these aids, in one way or another, and with varying degrees of success, help increase the independent mobility of visually impaired people, reducing self-produced confusion and allowing situational confusion to be more successfully dealt with (see Chapter 3, pages 21-24) (Golledge, 1991; Golledge *et al.*, 1991. For a full discussion of different navigation aids, see Jacobson and Kitchin, 1997).

Resolving NIMBY issues

In recent years we have seen the rise of NIMBY (not in my back yard) protests by people seeking to keep what they perceive as 'hazardous phenomena' away from the areas they live and interact in. One such 'hazardous phenomenon' is disabled people, and in particular people with developmental (e.g. Down's

Syndrome) and psychiatric (e.g. chronic depression, manic-depressive syndrome) impairments and people suffering from mental illness (e.g. schizophrenia). Indeed, there has been a general resistance by some sections of society to strategies of de-institutionalisation, care in the community, and the creation of an inclusive society. An example of resistance has been studied by Rob Wilton (1998), who explored the reaction of one particular community in Los Angeles to the sheltered accommodation of people with a history of mental illness. His research demonstrated that the protesters, who form a vocal minority, have used cultural representations and myths (see Chapter 4, pages 35-38) to create a moral panic (distrust) among the local non-disabled population. In particular, they have tried to persuade others in the neighbourhood that the residents of sheltered accommodation will devalue property, increase the inflow of other 'undesirable' groups such as homeless people, and pose a safety threat to children. The residents of the sheltered accommodation are also being used as scapegoats for all the ills of the neighbourhood, such as increasing unemployment. None of the protestors' claims have been backed by any concrete evidence.

The arguments of the NIMBY protesters are in direct conflict with the views of disabled people and their allies. They have been arguing, through the independent living movement, for an inclusive society that allows disabled people to live where and how they choose (see, for example, the Leonard Cheshire Foundation website, page 48). This means moving from the practice of segregation, charity and welfare to the practice of inclusion, employment and rights whereby non-disabled people accept disabled people for who they are and welcome them into their communities as valued and respected citizens.

Jenny Morris (1991) identifies four premises upon which the independent living movement is based:

1. All human life is of value.
2. Anyone, whatever their impairment, is capable of making choices.
3. People who are disabled by society's reaction to physical, sensory and intellectual impairment and to emotional distress have the right to assert control over their lives.
4. Disabled people have the right to full participation in society.

The points raised above reveal two competing sets of ideas. On the one hand disabled people and their allies want to see the building of an inclusive society, and on the other hand some non-disabled people want disabled people excluded from their neighbourhoods. As geographers, people who study communities within locales, we can play a part in helping to resolve these NIMBY conflicts. For example, geographers can expose the ways in which disabled people are being culturally represented. They can also collect data to enable comparisons to be made between places that have similar social characteristics, and to identify examples that back-up or refute protesters' claims. If examples are found that appear to back-up protesters' claims, geographers analyse them in an attempt to discover why the situation arose and what might be done to prevent something similar developing in other areas.
(Go to Activity Box 15.)

Photo: Leonard Cheshire.

Activity Box 15: Thinking about NIMBY issues

Consider the following types of building and the people who use them:

- a prison
- sheltered accommodation for people with a history of mental illness
- a hostel for homeless people
- a school for people with developmental (learning) difficulties
- a charity shop
- a day centre for people with physical and sensory impairments
- a youth club
- a centre for independent living
- a pub

For each example, consider the following:

1. Would you object to it being located in the area you live in? Rank the building uses in order of preference.
2. If you have objected to any forms of building use within your area, analyse the reasons that underlie your objection. Is your objection based upon cultural representations or documented evidence? Are there good reasons for objecting to the building being built in your local area?
3. If you have not objected to any forms of building use within your area, analyse the reasons that underlie your acceptance. Why is the building use acceptable to you?
4. If you were a person who needed or benefited from these services how would you feel if people objected to them?

List the class's answers to the four questions and discuss them as a class.

CHAPTER 6

TOWARDS AN INCLUSIVE SOCIETY

An implicit argument developed within this book has been that there is a need to build an inclusive society, that is a society which respects and values all its members, including disabled people, for who they are (Figure 17). This means moving beyond notions of assimilation (disabled people adapting to fit into non-disabled society), charity and sympathy to notions of inclusion and rights. Disabled people are often disabled by the fact that society in general, through its attitudes and actions, actively excludes them. Disabled people do not have the same access to what most people would consider basic rights such as education, housing, transport, employment and the built environment. The right of disabled people to take part in every aspect of society needs to be recognised and acted upon. There needs to be widespread changes in people's attitudes towards disabled people, and enforceable and wide-ranging legislation which requires all sections of society to cater for disabled customers and employees needs to be introduced. (Go to Activity Box 15.)

Figure 17: An inclusive society is one that values disabled people. Photos: Leonard Cheshire.

Activity Box 15: Creating an inclusive society

Think about and answer the following questions.

1. Would you think it was fair if you were denied access to education, shops or employment if you became disabled?
2. How does society need to change to become more inclusive in nature?
3. What sorts of actions should the government take to make society more inclusive, and why?
4. What role can geographers play in creating an inclusive society?
5. What role can *you* play in creating an inclusive society?

List the individual answers to these questions and discuss them as a class.

Using your answers, draw up a short manifesto to either:

a. justify society staying the same, or
b. justify society changing. If you think that society needs changing, briefly detail how it should change (list as bullet points).

The manifesto should take the form of a short pamphlet (four pages maximum).

In order for change to occur, people must act upon their convictions. Send your manifesto for change (if this is your decision) to the head of your school/college with a covering letter detailing how you think the school or college should change to become more inclusive. Include supporting evidence that highlights some of the main issues (e.g. an accessibility map, Figures 1-3, pages 17-18).

Becoming an ally

One role that we can all undertake to help create an inclusive society is to become an ally of disabled people. An ally is a member of the non-disabled community who takes a stand against ableism and the social injustices suffered by people with physical, sensory or mental impairments (Figure 18).

How active an ally you wish to be is a personal decision you need to make. It might mean offering practical help, or actively campaigning for disabled people's rights, or it might be expressed in how you live your own life. (Go to Activity Box 16).

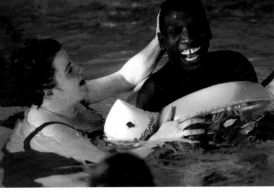

Figure 18: Allies of disabled people work to ensure that all members of society enjoy the same rights. Photos: Leonard Cheshire.

Activity Box 16: Becoming an ally of disabled people

1. Study this list of ally characteristics and decide whether you are an ally of disabled people.

An ally:

- listens to and respects the perspectives and experiences of disabled people
- acknowledges the privileges received from being non-disabled and works to ensure so that all members of society enjoy the same rights
- recognises that unlearning oppressive beliefs and actions is a lifelong process, not a single event, and welcomes each learning opportunity
- is willing to take risks, try new behaviours and act in spite of his or her own fear and the resistance from other non-disabled people
- acts against social injustice/ableism out of a belief that it is in her or his own self-interest to do so
- is willing to be confronted about their own behaviour and attitudes and consider changing them
- is committed to taking action against social injustice/ableism in his or her own sphere of influence
- believes she or he can make a difference by acting and speaking out against social injustice/ableism.

2. If you decide you are an ally, list all the ways you might help disabled people tackle ableism or if you decide you are not an ally explain why.

Compile a composite list from the responses of class members and discuss it as a class. Also discuss the non-ally responses.

3. Look at Figure 19 and decide which particular action category you currently occupy. Next decide which category you would like to occupy and describe how you might go about making the transformation between categories (assuming you want to change).

Compile three class lists (headed 'current', 'like to be', 'how to transform') and discuss each one.

Abridged from: Wejeyesinghe *et al.*, 1997, p. 108.

Final words

This book has explored the relationship between geography and disability. It is hoped that readers will have come to understand the main issues, and how geography is implicated in the lives of disabled people. It should be clear that, as geographers, we can contribute towards creating an inclusive society both through highlighting the ways in which disabled people are discriminated against and through providing practical and policy-orientated solutions that will improve the quality of life of some disabled people.

Initiating, preventing
Working to change individual and institutional actions and policies that discriminate against disabled people, planning educational programmes or other events, working for the passage of legislation that protects disabled people from discrimination, being explicit about making sure target group members are full participants in organisations or groups.

Supporting, encouraging
Supporting others who speak out against oppression or who are working to be more inclusive of disabled people by backing up others who speak out, forming allies group, joining a coalition.

Educating others
Moving beyond only educating self to question and dialogue with others too. Rather than only stopping oppressive comments or behaviours, also engages people in discussion to share reasons for objecting to a comment and action.

Educating self
Taking actions to learn more about oppression and the experiences and heritage of disabled people by reading, attending workshops, seminars, cultural events, participating in discussions, joining organisations or groups that oppose oppression, attending social action and change events.

Recognising, action
Is aware of oppression, recognises oppressive actions of self and others and takes action to stop it.

Recognising, no action
Is aware of oppressive actions by self or others and their harmful effects, but takes no action to stop this behaviour. This inaction is the result of fear, lack of information, confusion about what to do. Experiences discomfort at the contradiction between awareness and action.

Denying
Enabling oppression by denying that disabled people are oppressed. Does not actively oppress, but by denying that oppression exists, colludes with oppression.

Actively participating
Telling oppressive jokes, putting down disabled people, intentionally avoiding disabled people, discriminating against disabled people, verbally or physically harassing disabled people.

CONFRONTING OPPRESSION

SUPPORTING OPPRESSION

Figure 19: Action continuum.

REFERENCES AND FURTHER READING

References

Barnes, C. (1992) *Cabbage Syndrome: The social construction of dependence.* Lewis: Falmer.

Barton, L. (1996) 'Sociology and disability: some emerging issues' in Barton, L. (ed) *Disability and Society: Emerging issues and insights.* Harlow: Longman, pp. 3-17.

Berthoud, R. (1995) 'Social security, poverty and disabled people' in Zarb, G. (ed) *Removing Disabling Barriers.* London: Policy Studies Institute, pp. 77-87.

Berthoud, R., Lakey, J. and McKay, S. (1993) *The Economic Problems of Disabled People.* London: PSI Publishing.

Clark-Carter, D.D., Heyes, A.D. and Howarth, C.I. (1986) 'The efficiency and walking speed of visually impaired pedestrians', *Ergonomics*, 29, pp. 779-89.

Department of the Environment and Local Government (1999) *Consultation Document. Revision of Part M: Building Regulations.* Dublin: DoELG.

Elton, B. (1992) *Gridlock.* London: MacDonald.

Ewart, K. (1998) personal communication, Centre for University Accessibility, University of Ulster.

Gill, B. and Loughman, C. (no date) *Exploring Contemporary Issues: A guide to teaching.* (Social Education Course: Leaving Certificate Applied). Dublin: Combat Poverty Agency/National Committee for Development Education/The Leaving Certificate Applied Support Services.

Golledge, R.G. (1991) 'Tactical strip maps as navigational aids', *Journal of Visual Impairment and Blindness,* 85, 7, pp. 296-301.

Golledge, R.G. (1993) 'Geography and the disabled: a survey with special reference to vision impaired and blind populations', *Transactions of the Institute of British Geographers,* 18, pp. 63-85.

Golledge, R.G., Loomis, J.M., Klatzky, R.L., Flury, A. and Yang, X-L. (1991) 'Designing a personal guidance system to aid navigation without sight: progress on the GIS component', *International Journal of Geographical Information Systems,* 5, pp. 373-96.

Hardiman, R. and Jackson, B.W. (1997) 'Conceptual foundations for social justice courses' in Adams, M., Bell, L.A. and Griffin, P. (eds) *Teaching for Diversity and Social Justice.* London: Routledge, pp. 16-29.

Imrie, R. (1996) *Disability in the City: International perspectives.* London: Paul Chapman Publishing.

Irish Wheelchair Association (1994) *People First.* Dublin: Irish Wheelchair Association.

Jacobson, R.D. and Kitchin, R.M. (1997) 'Geographical information systems and people with visual impairments or blindness: exploring the potential to education, orientation and navigation', *Transactions in Geographical Information Systems,* 2, 4, pp. 315-32.

Kitchin, R. and Mulcahy, F. (1999) *Disability, Access to Education and Future Opportunities.* Dublin: Combat Poverty Agency.

Kitchin, R.M., Jacobson, R.D., Golledge, R.G. and Blades, M. (1998a) 'Belfast without sight', *Irish Geography,* 31, pp. 34-46.

Kitchin, R., Shirlow, P. and Shuttleworth, I. (1998b) 'On the margins: disabled peoples' experiences of employment in Donegal, west Ireland', *Disability and Society,* 13, pp. 785-806.

Labour Force Survey (1992) *Labour Force Survey.* London: HMSO.

Lamb, B. and Layzell, S. (1994) *Disabled in Britain: A world apart.* London: Scope.

Martin, J., White, A. and Meltzer, H. (1989) *Disabled Adults: Services, transport and employment.* London: HMSO.

Milligan, C. (1997) 'Bearing the burden: a geography of caring'. Paper presented at ENRGHI 97, Queen Mary and Westfield College, University of London, 1-2 July.

Morris, J. (1991) *Pride Against Prejudice: Transforming the attitudes to disability.* London: The Women's Press.

Morris, J. (1993) *Independent Lives - Community care and disabled people.* Basingstoke: MacMillan.

Napolitano, S. (1995) 'Mobility impairment' in Hales, G. (ed) *Beyond Disability: Towards an enabling environment.* London: Sage, pp. 30-5.

NRB (1998) *Building for All.* Dublin: NRB.

Oliver, M. (1990) *The Politics of Disablement.* Basingstoke: MacMillan.

Philo, C. (1987) ' "Fit localities for an asylum": the historical geography of the "mad-business" in England viewed through the pages of the *Asylum Journal*', *Journal of Historical Geography,* 13, pp. 398-415.

Pitzele, S. (1995) 'Chronic illness, disability and sexuality in people older than fifty', *Sexuality and Disability,* 13, 4, pp. 309-25.

Rauscher, L. and McClintock, M. (1997) 'Ableism curriculum design' in Adams, M., Bell, L.A. and Griffin, P. (eds) *Teaching for Diversity and Social Justice.* London: Routledge, pp. 198-230.

Sibley, D. (1995) *Geographies of Exclusion: Society and difference in the West.* London: Routledge.

Thompson, P., Lavery, M. and Curtice, J. (1990) *Short-changed by Disability.* Disablement Income Group.

Vujakovic, P. and Matthews, M.H. (1994) 'Contorted, folded, torn: environmental values, cartographic representation and the politics of disability', *Disability and Society*, 9, pp. 359-75.

Waxman, B.F. and Finger, A. (1991) 'The politics of sexuality, reproduction and disability', *Sexuality Update, National Task Force on Sexuality and Disability*, 4, 1, pp. 1-3.

Wejeyesinghe, C.L., Griffin, P. and Love, B. (1997) 'Racism curriculum design' in Adams, M., Bell, L.A. and Griffin, P. (eds) *Teaching for Diversity and Social Justice.* London: Routledge, pp. 82-109.

Wilton, R. (1998) '*Those* people ... community opposition to group homes as fear of difference'. Paper presented at the conference of the Association of American Geographers, Boston, 25-29 March.

Young, I.M. (1990) *Justice and the Politics of Difference.* Princeton NJ: Princeton University Press.

Further reading

Books

Most writing on disability and geography is academic in nature and written for other 'experts'. However, the following books provide good, if relatively advanced, further reading:

Butler, R. and Parr, H. (eds) (2000) *Mind and Body Spaces.* London: Routledge.

Gleeson, B. (1999) *Geographies of Disability.* London: Routledge.

Imrie, R. (1996) *Disability and the City: International perspectives.* London: Paul Chapman Publishing.

Accessible books concerning geography and exclusion include:

Jackson, P. (1989) *Maps of Meaning.* London: Routledge

Sibley, D. (1995) *Geographies of Exclusion: Society and difference in the West.* London: Routledge.

Other useful texts include:

Campbell, J. and Oliver, M. (1996) *Disability Politics: Understanding our past, changing our future.* London: Routledge.

Drake, R.F. (1999) *Understanding Disability Policies.* Basingstoke: MacMillan.

Linton, S. (1998) *Claiming Disability: Knowledge and identity.* New York: New York University Press.

Oliver, M. (1990) *The Politics of Disablement.* Basingstoke: MacMillan.

Oliver, M. (1996) *Understanding Disability: From theory to practice.* Basingstoke: MacMillan.

Pointon, A. and Davies, C. (1997) *Framed: Interrogating disability in the media.* London: British Film Institute.

Saraga, E. (1998) *Embodying the Social: Constructions of difference.* London: Routledge.

Websites

The Disability and Geography International Network (DAGIN) site provides references to specific papers: http://www.swansea.ac.uk/disability/dagin/ and other websites worth investigating are:

- AbilityNet: http://www.abilitynet.co.uk
- ADAPT: http://www.adapt.org/
- Centre for Accessible Environments: http://www.cae.org.uk
- Disability Net: http://www.disabilitynet.co.uk/
- Disability People's International: http://www.escape.ca/~dpi/accestxt.html
- Disability Research Unit: http://www.leeds.ac.uk/sociology/dru/dru.html
- Disability Rights Commission: http://www.disability.gov.uk/drc/
- International Disability News Ticker: http://www.abilityinfo.com/ticker.html
- Joseph Rowntree Foundation: www.jrf.org.uk
- Leonard Cheshire Foundation: http://www.leonard-cheshire.org
- National Rehabilitation Board: http://www.cais.com/naric/
- Scope: http://www.scope.org.uk
- Yahoo links: http://www.yahoo.com/Society_and_Culture/Disabilities/